BUCKET OR F*CK IT LIST

Michael O'Mara Books Limited

This paperback edition first published in 2026

First published in Great Britain in 2026 by
Michael O'Mara Books Limited
9 Lion Yard
Tremadoc Road
London SW4 7NQ

EU representative:
Authorised Rep Compliance Ltd
Ground Floor
71 Baggot Street Lower
Dublin D02 P593
Ireland

Copyright © Joy Gift Publishing Ltd 2026

All rights reserved. You may not copy, store, distribute, transmit, reproduce or otherwise make available this publication (or any part of it) in any form, or by any means (electronic, digital, optical, mechanical, photocopying, recording, machine readable, text/data mining or otherwise), without the prior written permission of the publisher. Any person who does any unauthorized act in relation to this publication may be liable to criminal prosecution and civil claims for damages.

A CIP catalogue record for this book is available from the British Library.

Papers used by Michael O'Mara Books Limited are natural, recyclable products made from wood grown in sustainable forests. The manufacturing processes conform to the environmental regulations of the country of origin.

ISBN: 978-1-78929-883-3 in paperback print format

1 2 3 4 5 6 7 8 9 10

Cover design by Milestone Creative
Designed and typeset Bag of Badgers Ltd
Printed and bound in China

www.mombooks.com

For further information see www.mombooks.com/about/sustainability-climate-focus
Report any safety issues to product.safety@mombooks.com

CONTENTS

Your no bullsh*t breakdown

	How to use this book	5
1.	Friends like these	7
2.	Control freakery	13
3.	Me, me, me	19
4.	Let go of the past	25
5.	FOMO	31
6.	Sorry (not sorry)	37
7.	Let it out	43
8.	Stop overthinking	49
9.	Take a break	55
10.	Can you fix it?	61
11.	File a complaint	67
12.	The dating game	73
13.	Thanks for the invite ...	79
14.	Message incoming	85
15.	Embrace failure	91
16.	In pursuit of perfection	97
17.	Be yourself	103
18.	Just say no	109
19.	The last word	115
20.	What next?	121

'To change one's life: start immediately. Do it flamboyantly. No exceptions.'

William James

HOW TO USE THIS BOOK

This book shows you how to do the good stuff in life and how to let go of the cr✻p.

Use the journal prompts to focus your attention on finding the dead weight in your life. By pinpointing your bad habits, negative thoughts and unproductive behaviours, you can identify what's standing in the way of you becoming a happier, less stressed-out human being. You can then work out how to shift and reframe your approach to life's flashpoints so they don't keep dragging you down.

When you get stuck and need help navigating the cr✻p, use one of the no-fuss, tell-it-like-it-is flowcharts to show you the way.

When you let go of the dead weight, you make space to focus on what you love and want to celebrate in life. So, be kind to yourself and stop wasting precious time – learn to say, 'F✻ck it.'

FRIENDS LIKE THESE

As humans, we naturally want to make connections with other people. When you make a connection with the right person, it can have a hugely positive impact on your life. You boost each other's energy levels and self-esteem, and you laugh until your sides ache. If you make a connection that doesn't give you that, think about if it's something you want in your life. It's okay for relationships to ebb and flow, but sometimes friendships simply stop serving you.

THE GOOD, THE BAD AND THE UGLY

Understand what you value in a friendship and what it should (and shouldn't) bring into your life.

Step 1: The check-in
How are my current friendships working?

These qualities make someone a great friend
_____
_____
_____

Things that make friendships hard work
_____
_____
_____

How I feel when I'm not looking forward to meeting up with certain friends
_____
_____
_____
_____

Step 2: The shift
What can I do to move away from unhelpful, energy-sapping friendships?

These are the friends I feel incompatible with

_____
_____
_____

The friendships aren't working any more because

_____
_____
_____

How I would feel without these friends in my life

_____
_____
_____

Reaffirm what you want from your friendships.

I am choosing friends who make me feel

_____

I am choosing to let go of friends who make me feel

_____

F*CK IT TOP TIPS

How to say farewell to toxic friends

* Be honest and keep it to the point. Think about how they treat you and how that makes you feel – you don't owe them a detailed explanation.

* If you don't feel able to tell someone explicitly that you don't want to be friends with them, you can gradually distance yourself. Keep yourself busy elsewhere with other friends and let time do the work.

* Distancing yourself can take time, so be patient. Once you have communicated your feelings, don't be afraid to block them on social media and delete their number from your phone.

* Resist the urge to re-engage on any level. They may try to win you back or punish you by making your life difficult. Ditching a friend is a tough thing to do, but it's time to stop letting them control your life.

F*CK IT FLOWCHART

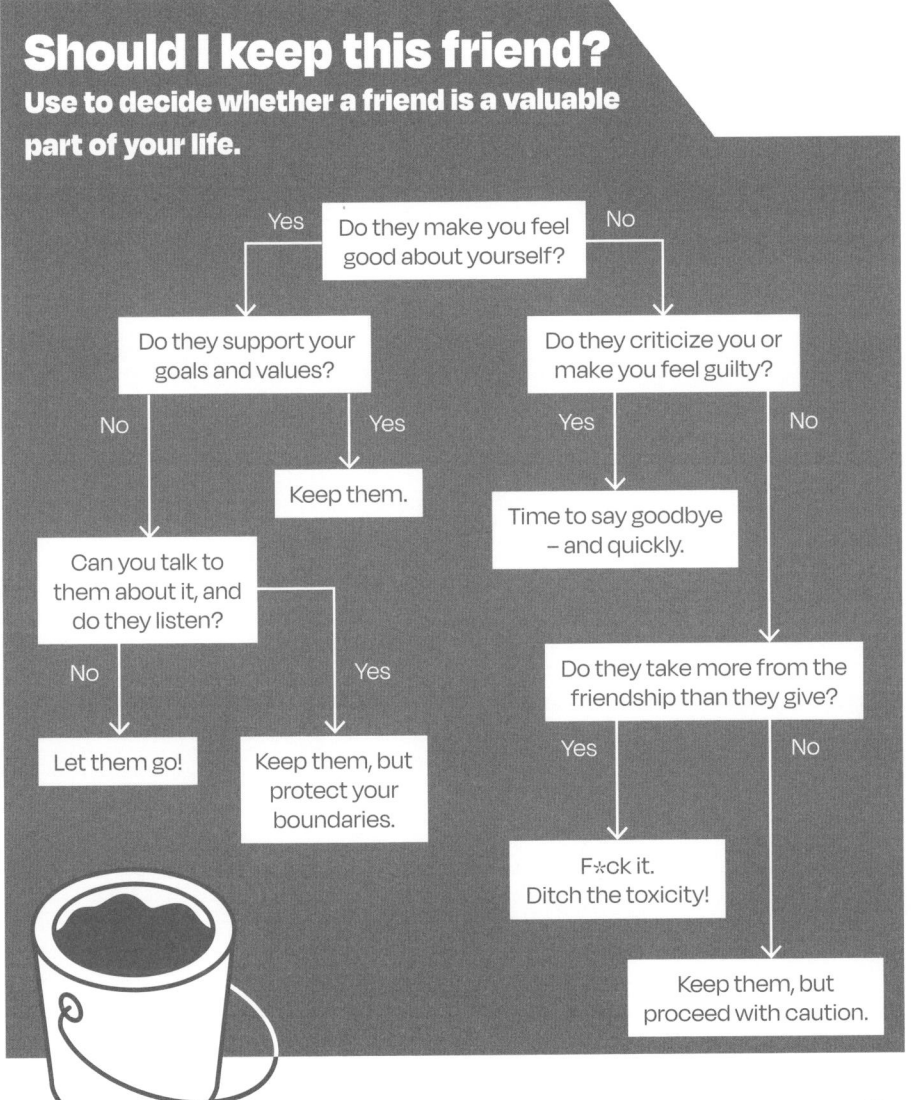

CONTROL FREAKERY

Do you know someone who doesn't get fazed by anything? They meet life's challenges with their game face on; they give a shrug and move on to something else. They've learned to not worry about things that are outside their control. When you start to focus on things you can control and let go those you can't, it's a liberating experience. Stop being a control freak and give it a go.

THE ART OF LETTING GO

Decide what you can do something about and what is a waste of your brain space and energy.

Step 1: The check-in
What's keeping me awake at night?

The things I am most worried about at the moment

How these worries make me feel

How would I feel if I was free of these worries?

Step 2: The shift
When I recognize what I can't change and invest my energy in what I can ...

What I can't change and can let go of

_____
_____
_____

What I can influence or control

_____
_____
_____

Steps I can take to start to change the things within my control

_____
_____
_____

Consider what you can't directly change but can influence. List the skills you need to make this happen

_____
_____
_____
_____

F*CK IT TOP TIPS

What you can and can't control

1. What I can't control:

- Other people's behaviour.
- Whether other people like me.
- The past/things that have already happened.
- Circumstances.

2. What I can't directly control but can influence:

- The direction of a situation.
- The people in my life/who I spend time with.
- My health, work and relationships.

3. What I can control:

- My own actions and decisions.
- My behaviours and the words I use.
- My reactions.

The only thing you have direct control over is yourself. You can't do anything about the other sh*t. Shift your focus and energy to the things you can influence and control.

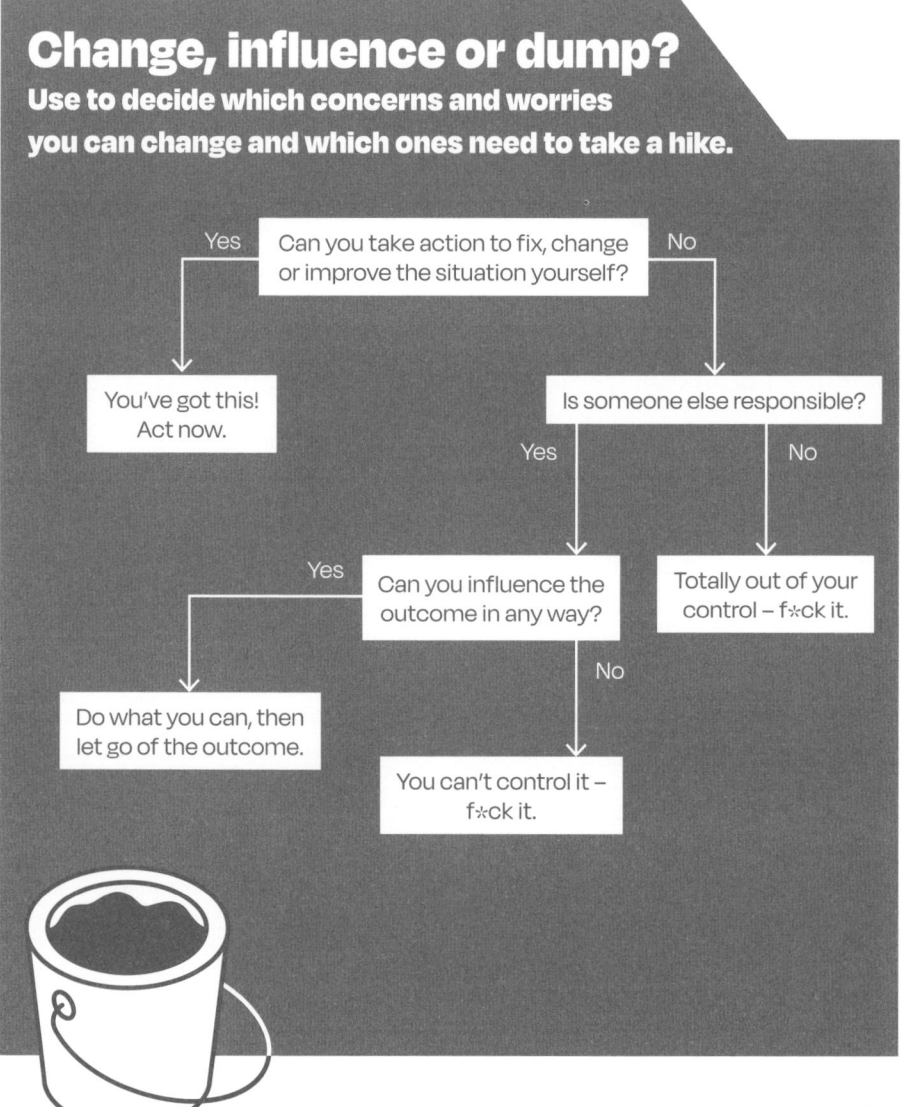

ME, ME, ME

Do you think you're being selfish if you put yourself first? There's a big difference between not giving two hoots about other people and choosing to prioritize your own time and well-being. When you feel good about life, your relationships are better and the benefits extend to everyone around you. So, no – putting your own needs, wants and desires first isn't selfish. Do something that lights you up. Choose joy!

JOY OVER JUSTIFICATION

Choose what lights you up – not what makes sense to everyone else.

Step 1: The check-in
What am I doing that puts me at the bottom of the list?

Activities I feel obliged to do
___
___
___

Roles/hobbies I feel I have to explain or defend
___
___
___

Choices I've made to avoid judgement, rather than because they're right for me
___
___
___
___

Step 2: The shift
If joy was my priority ...

Things that make me feel alive
_____
_____
_____
_____

Things I'd do even if no one clapped or cared
_____
_____
_____
_____

Something I want to try that I know others will frown at
_____
_____
_____
_____

Now, circle one thing from each list above and reframe it.

Instead of _____
because I should, I'm choosing _____
because it makes me feel _____

F*CK IT PLAN

Boost your joy

Now that you know it's okay to say 'f*ck it', and choose joy over justification, expand your horizons!

I will try these things I've always wanted to experience

Things that bring me joy I can share with a loved one

Big, joyful experiences I need to start saving for!

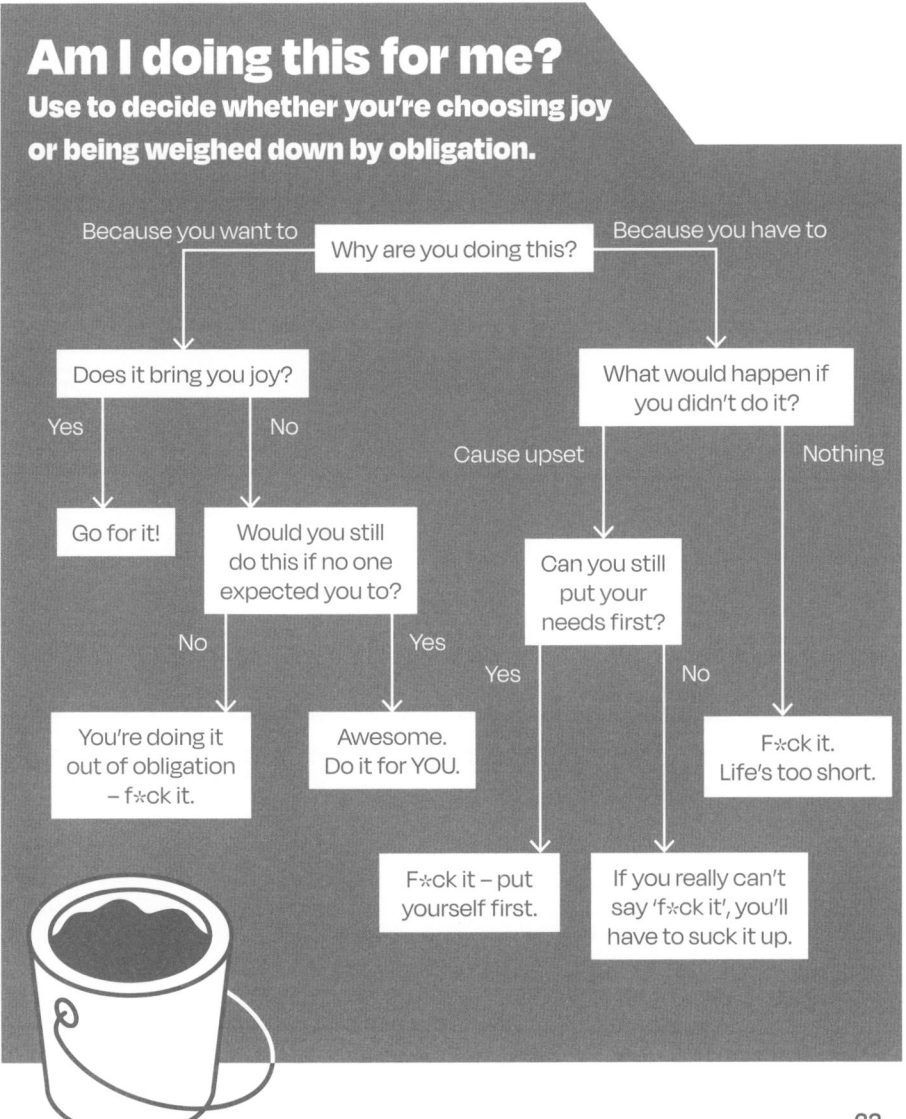

LET GO OF THE PAST

There's one thing for sure: you can't change what has happened in the past. But that doesn't stop the past rearing its big, ugly head when you're trying to get on with your life. Past experiences are good to hold on to if they have a positive impact on your present and future. For a lighter life, it's those things in the past that you carry like a rock on your shoulders that you need to ditch.

STOP HOLDING ON – LET GO!

Letting go of the past doesn't mean forgetting – it sets you free.

Step 1: The check-in
Looking back ...

Past situations I still feel are unresolved
_____
_____
_____

A lesson I learned the hard way
_____
_____
_____

What story do I tell myself about my past? Is it helping or hindering me?
_____
_____
_____

Step 2: The shift
Looking forward ...

How it would feel to release things in the past that weigh me down

_____
_____
_____

Things in the past I feel ready to start letting go of

_____
_____
_____

A moment from my past that shows my inner strength and resilience

_____
_____
_____

Now, choose one situation from the past and reframe it.

I am letting go of _____
and how it makes me feel. Instead, I feel grateful that it taught me _____

F*CK IT TOP TIPS

Write a letter to your younger self

If you could write a letter to a younger version of yourself, what would you want them to know? What would you tell them to say 'f*ck it' to, and what would you tell them to embrace and enjoy?

Dear Me,

With love from,

Me

F*CK IT FLOWCHART

Use it or dump it?
Use to decide what experiences from the past aren't serving you in the present.

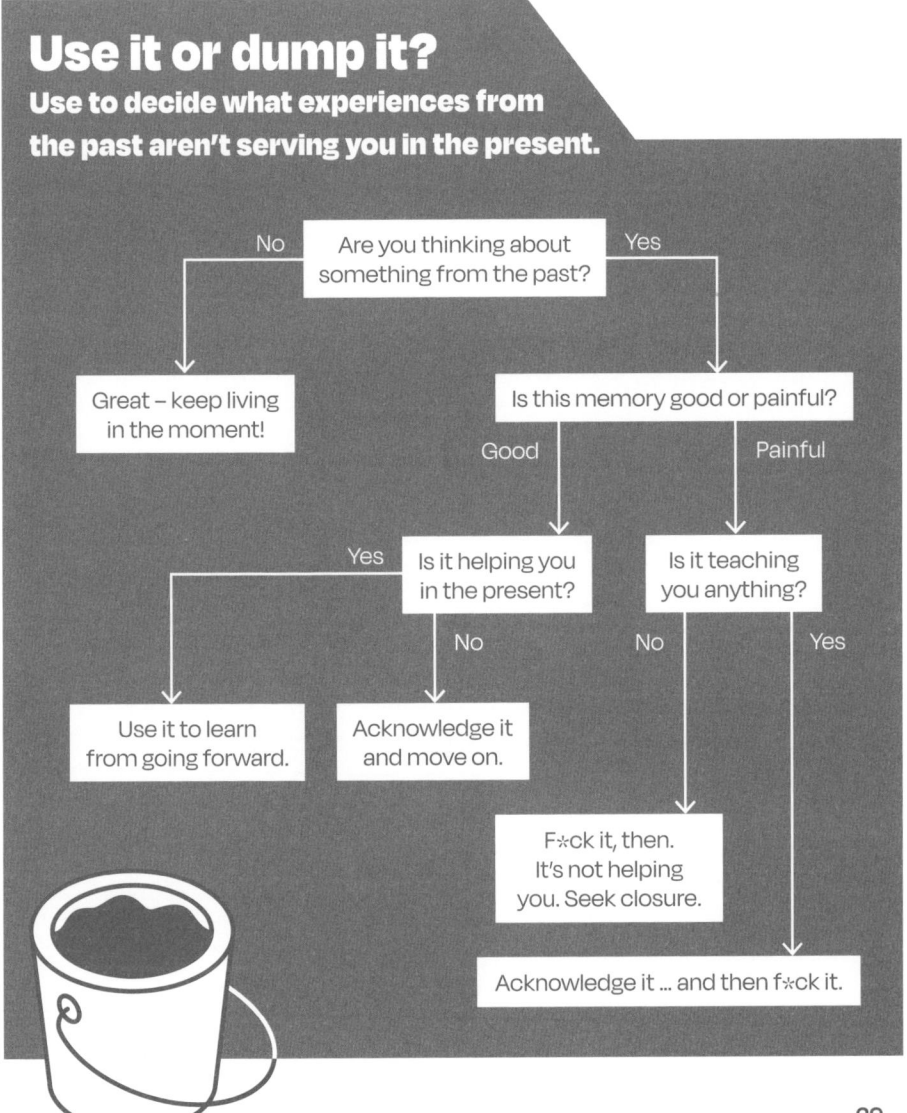

FOMO

The fear of missing out. Ah, everyone gets a bit of FOMO from time to time. It's natural – unless it makes you that annoying person who constantly butts into conversations, turns up at every event (invited or uninvited) and who has 50k 'friends' on social media. But what if you're so worried you're going to miss out that you don't have time for the things that you really want to do? Get a life … and make sure it's your own.

Find out what really floats your boat and ditch worrying about what everyone else is doing.

Step 1: The check-in
What do I think I'm missing out on?

Situations or people that most trigger my FOMO

What I think I gain by being part of everything

Things for myself that I'm missing out on because of FOMO

Step 2: The shift
When I reframe FOMO ...

Things I have gained by saying no in the past
___
___

How I would feel if I trusted that I'm exactly where I need to be
___
___

Three things I can say no to now and know I won't be missing out
___
___

Now, imagine ... How would a fulfilling day, regardless of what others are doing, look for you?
___
___
___
___
___
___

F✻CK IT TOP TIPS

JOMO – the joy of missing out

JOMO ... the perfect way to put FOMO on your f✻ck it list. It focuses on taking pleasure in not doing something and not trying to keep up with the crowd. Here's how to enjoy the positive impact of JOMO.

✻ **Know your own priorities.** What truly matters to you? What and who brings joy into your life? If something doesn't align with your priorities – f✻ck it.

✻ **Limit your time on social media.** Less scrolling through other people's lives (which, in reality, are exceedingly dull) lets you focus on your own life and what makes you happy. Try checking your feeds only once or twice a day and for a maximum of ten minutes.

✻ **Schedule in time for solo activities.** Reading, gardening, movies – whatever you find calming and fulfilling and makes you feel like you.

✻ **Be grateful for the present and you'll be less likely to feel you're missing out.** What in your life makes you thankful? Say a big 'thank you' and pat yourself on the back for all the good stuff – everything else can just f✻ck off.

F*CK IT FLOWCHART

Choose JOMO over FOMO
Use this to understand your FOMO/JOMO thought process..

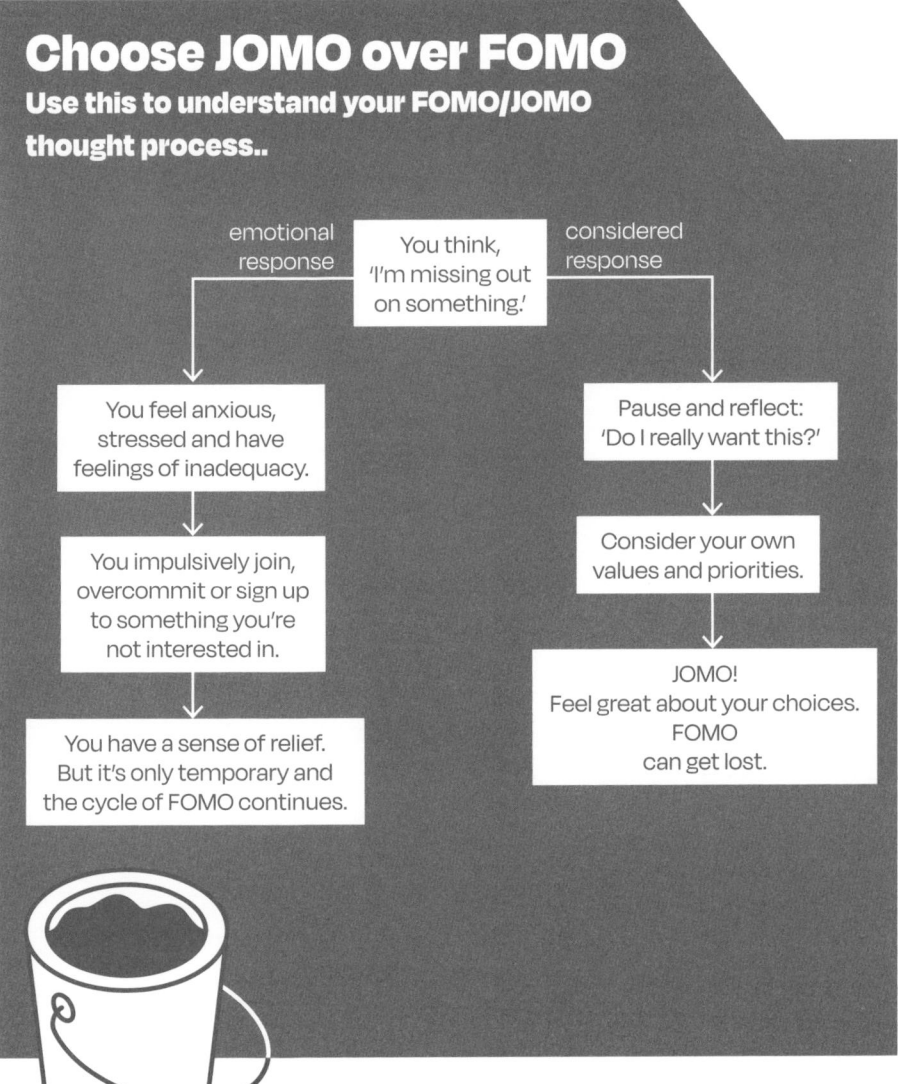

SORRY (NOT SORRY)

No one really likes to apologize. For such a short word, 'sorry' can be extremely painful. As a child, you get away with pretty much everything just by saying sorry; as an adult, it's much more complicated. Overuse the word 'sorry' and it starts to mean nothing at all. It's a minefield! All the more reason why you should only apologize when necessary – and when you mean it.

Be mindful about what you're apologizing for, why and whether it's necessary.

Step 1: The check-in
Am I saying sorry for the right reasons?

What currently guides my decision whether or not to apologize

---

Times I've apologized just to avoid conflict or guilt

What I consider before choosing to apologize

People I owe an apology but haven't reached out to yet

_____

_____

Things I will no longer apologize for

_____

_____

How not apologizing for things I'm not responsible for makes me feel

_____

_____

Remember that you can't control other people's behaviour. Don't feel compelled to apologize on behalf of others. Instead, try reframing.

I understand that [name] was wrong when they

_____

They need to take responsibility for their behaviour and

_____

F*CK IT
DOS AND DON'Ts

If you genuinely do need to apologize ...

DO:

- ☑ Accept responsibility for what's happened.
- ☑ Directly apologize for what you've done and the impact it had.
- ☑ Think about what you can do to fix it or stop it happening again.

DON'T:

- ☒ Apologize in a way that accepts responsibility but expresses no remorse.
- ☒ Make the apology all about what you're feeling (rather than how the other person feels).
- ☒ Simultaneously apologize and retract responsibility – 'I'm sorry, but ...'

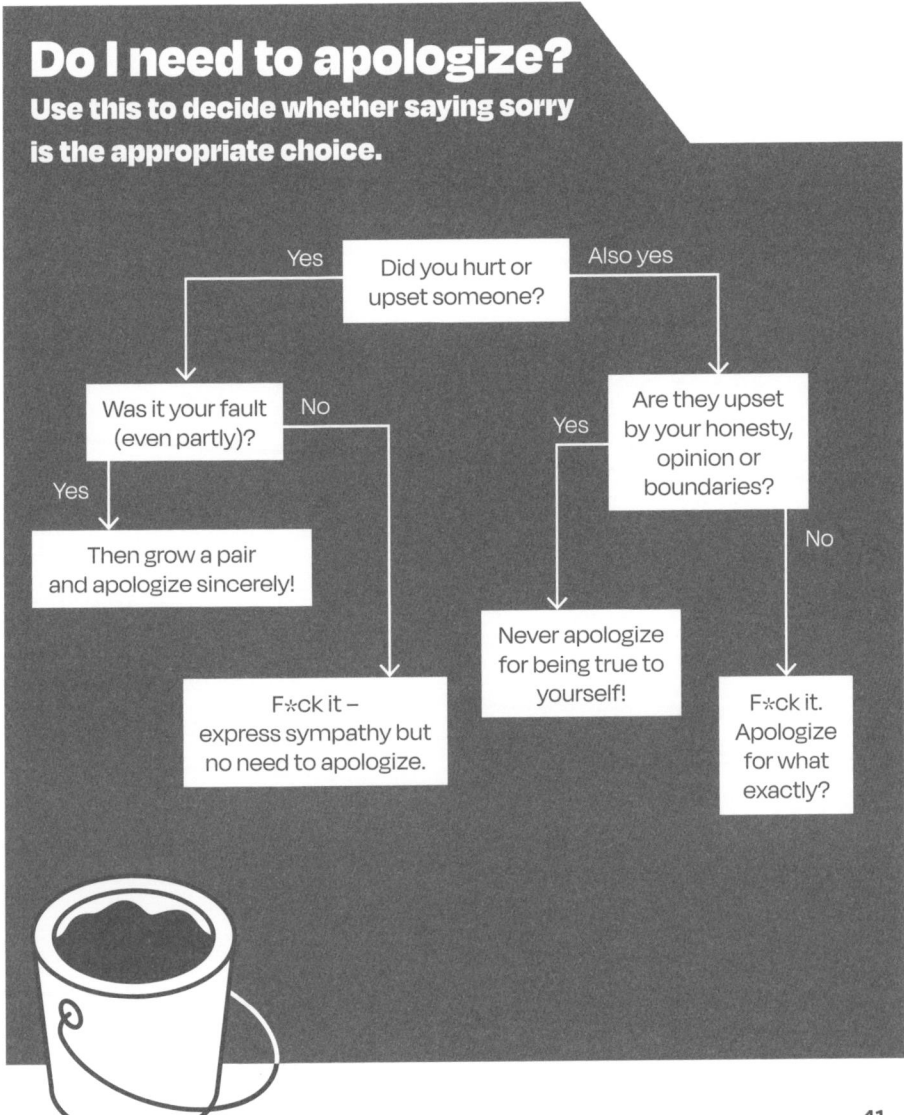

LET IT OUT

Do you keep how you feel to yourself?
Being honest about your emotions doesn't mean blurting out what's on your mind without considering the impact. It means not holding on to your feelings so they start to fester inside you. When you suppress emotions, you damage your own well-being as well as your relationships with others. Time to drop the mask and be true to yourself – your feelings count.

Choose to say how you feel without fear of being misunderstood.

Step 1: The check-in
What I'm currently keeping inside ...

Emotions I tend to suppress or hide

___

What I think will happen if I stop hiding how I feel

___

How hiding my feelings affects my personal and work relationships

___

Emotions I most want to express

_____
_____
_____

Gentle ways to begin sharing how I feel

_____
_____
_____

By expressing my feelings freely, my life would feel

_____
_____
_____

Create a positive affirmation for encouragement.

Example: 'I can express my feelings openly and honestly. My emotions are valid and I deserve to be heard.'

_____
_____
_____
_____

F*CK IT TOP TIPS

Top conversation openers

You've decided to bite the bullet and say how you really feel. If you don't know how to get the words out, try these opening lines ...

1. 'I've been struggling to cope lately with how I feel about ... '

2. 'I find it hard to share what I feel, but I think it would be helpful ... '

3. 'Can I share something that's been on my mind lately?'

4. 'I'm feeling stressed about ... '

5. 'I'm feeling frustrated with ... '

6. 'I'm feeling overwhelmed by ...'

7. 'I feel [insert emotion] when ...'

8. 'I'd like to talk about _____ with you ... '

F*CK IT FLOWCHART

Should I put my cards on the table?

Use for deciding when to let it all out.

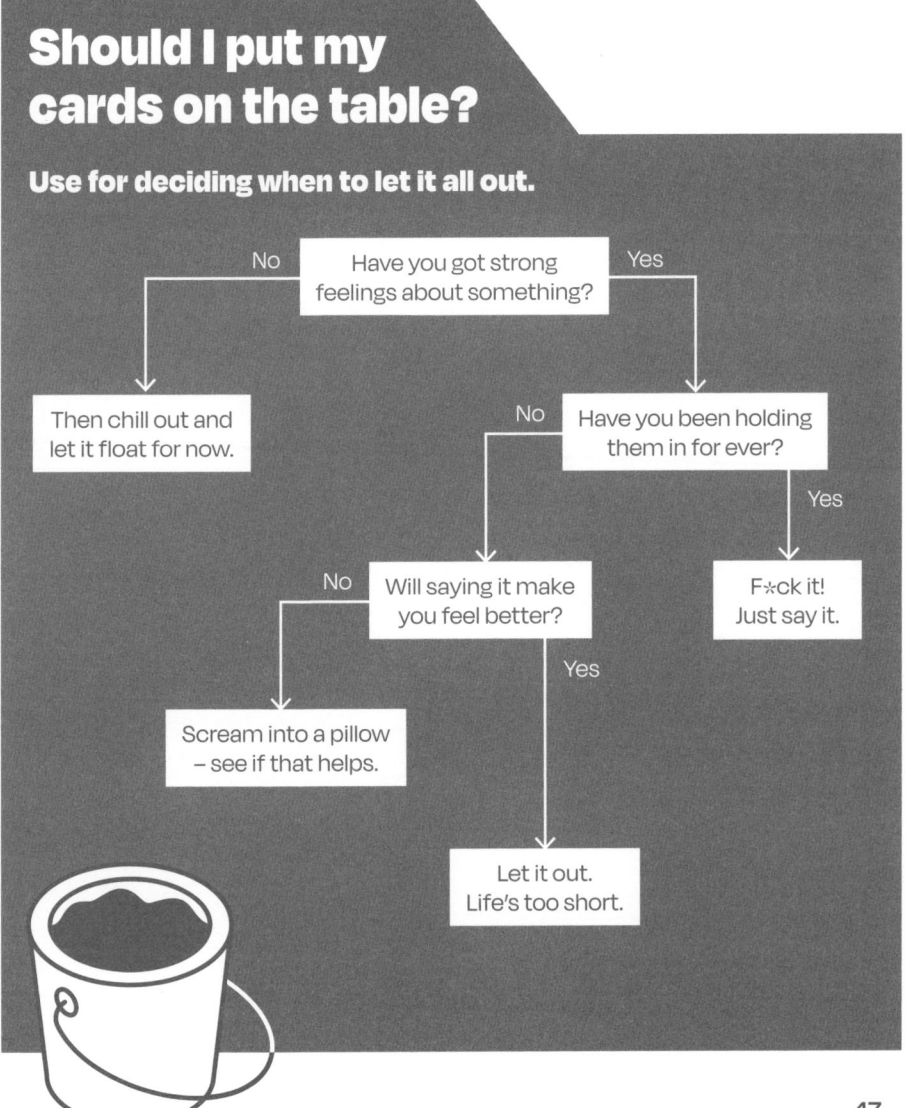

STOP OVERTHINKING

If you're prone to overthinking everything, even the simplest decision sets your mind racing. Once the momentum gets going and your thoughts spiral, it can be incredibly hard to put the brakes on. But you can. Sometimes, you have to say 'f*ck it' and take the plunge. Worry less – it's a sure-fire way to start enjoying your life more.

HELTER-SKELTER THINKING

Your overthinking brain wants to travel off in multiple directions and visit every scenario and disastrous outcome. STOP!

Step 1: The check-in
Am I caught in a spiral of overthinking?

What am I overthinking right now?
_____
_____
_____

Things I've missed out on because I overthought them
_____
_____
_____

Overthinking makes me feel
_____
_____
_____

Step 2: The shift
If I break the cycle of overthinking ...

How it would feel to trust myself rather than overthinking

Things I would do if I didn't overthink

A decision I can make now without overthinking it

Challenge a what-if thought with positive outcomes.

What if

A more realistic, positive outcome is

F*CK IT DOs AND DON'Ts

Stop overthinking in its tracks

DO:

- ☑ Write your thoughts down. What are you worried about? What's the evidence for and against your worry.
- ☑ Step away and do something different. Taking a break and shifting your focus is a great way to stop racing thoughts.
- ☑ Acknowledge you're overthinking – the quicker you can nip it in the bud, the better. Tell yourself it's 'just a thought/unnecessary worry' and it will lose its anxiety-inducing power.

DON'T:

- ☒ Engage in self-talk that reinforces negative feelings. For example: 'It will all go horribly wrong'; 'I'm not clever enough to do that.'
- ☒ Assume that experiences from the past will repeat themselves and affect the present and future.

F*CK IT FLOWCHART

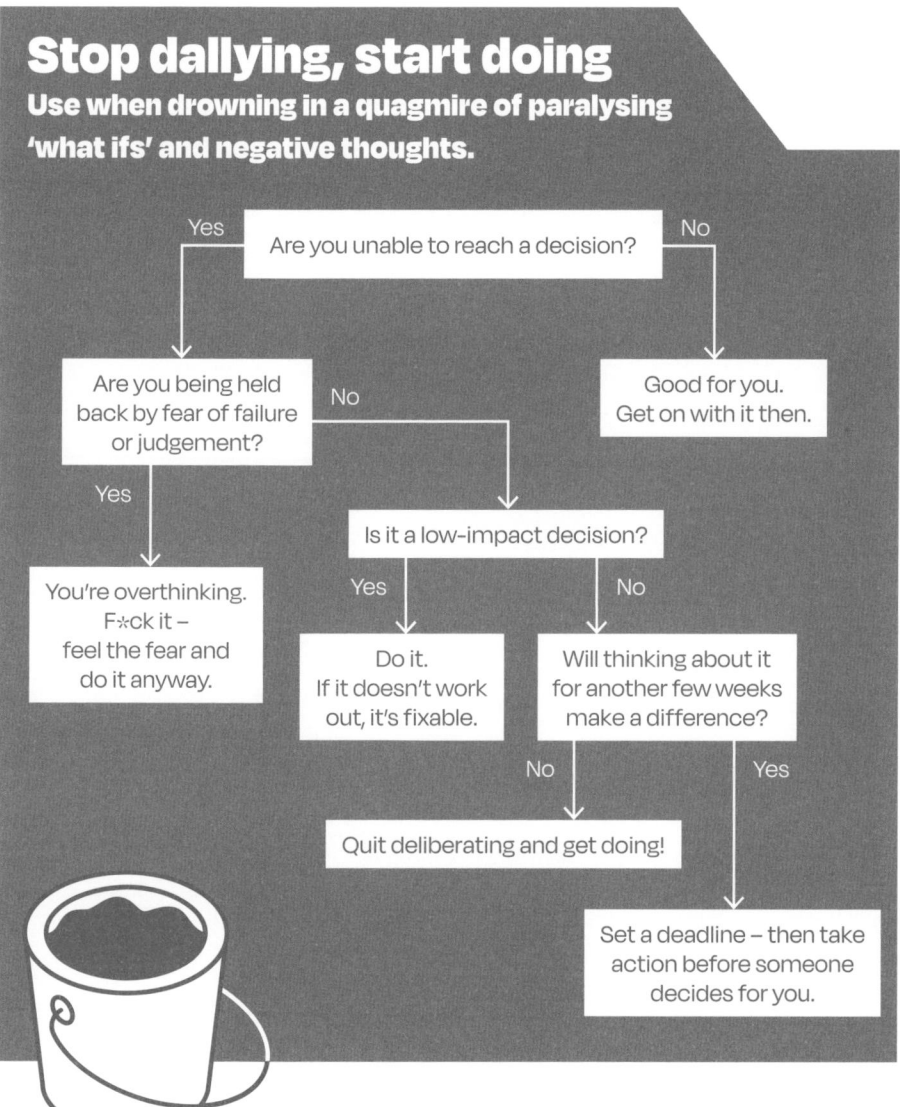

TAKE A BREAK

Taking time for yourself is the ultimate boost for your mental and physical health.
It is absolutely vital that you spend time relaxing, recharging and recuperating. In a world that rarely slows down for you, it's up to you to step off the treadmill and prioritize your self-care. So, why do you feel so guilty about it? Say 'f*ck it' and put yourself first.

CHOOSE TIME OUT OVER BURNOUT

Make the decision to look after yourself. It's the most important thing you can do.

Step 1: The check-in
How good am I at unadulterated self-care?

The last time I felt properly rested
_____
_____
_____

How I feel when I say no to something and allow myself to have some me-time
_____
_____
_____

Areas of my life where I'm doing too much
_____
_____
_____

Step 2: The shift
Putting my well-being first looks like …

How I can schedule time to switch off and relax
_____
_____
_____

Activities that relax me (and new ones I'd like to try)
_____
_____
_____

Boundaries I can set to prioritize my well-being
_____
_____
_____

Write a note to remind yourself why it's okay to take a break.

_____
_____
_____
_____
_____

F*CK IT
DOs AND DON'Ts

Make me-time work

DO:

- ☑ Set boundaries. If someone/something encroaches on your me-time, learn to say, 'No.'
- ☑ Make self-care a habit. Start by focusing on something you already do, and make more of it.
- ☑ Turn off notifications – better still, switch your phone off completely.

DON'T:

- ☒ Feel guilty about taking a break. You don't need to earn the right, you deserve it.
- ☒ Compromise your me-time just to please other people, especially at the cost of your own well-being.
- ☒ Scroll mindlessly. It's an immense waste of time and increases FOMO.

F*CK IT FLOWCHART

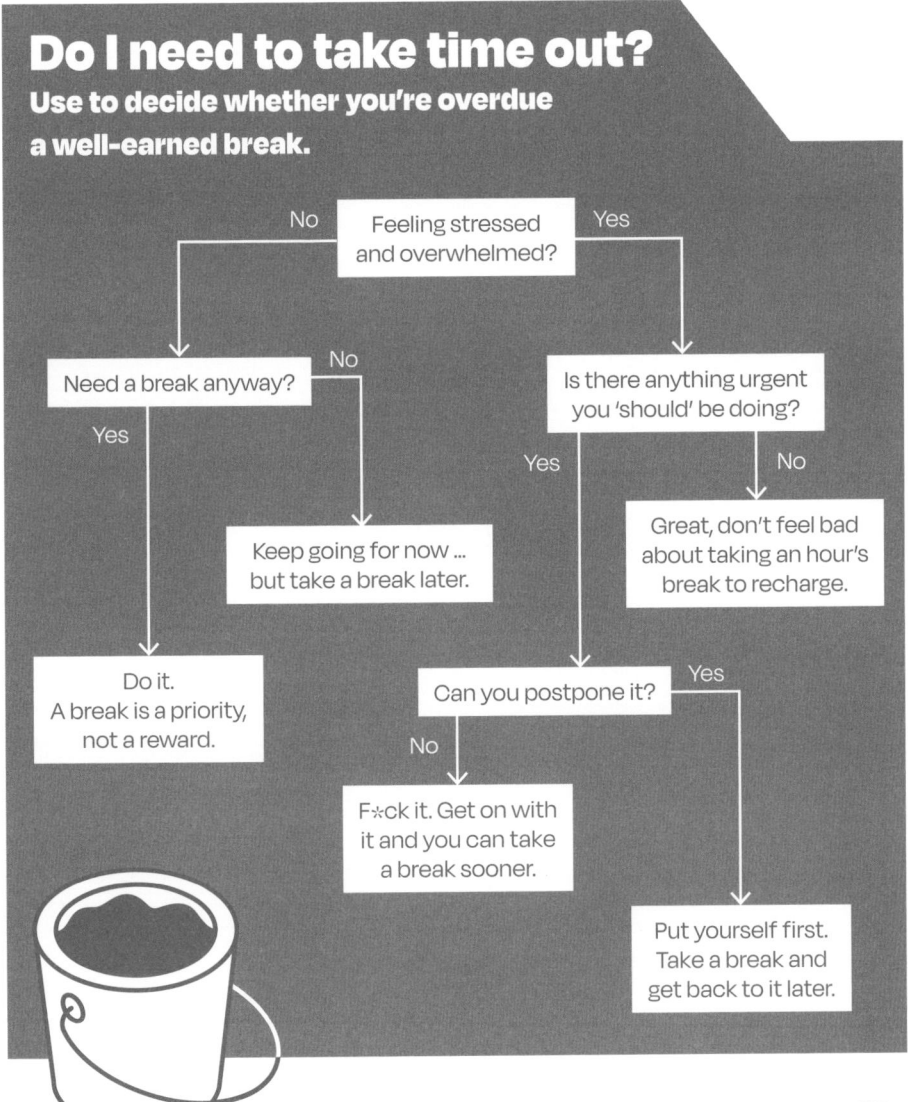

CAN YOU FIX IT?

Do you take on other people's problems?
You might not be a people pleaser, but you could be a 'fixer' with buckets of empathy who doesn't like to see people struggling. Sometimes, you need to acknowledge that something isn't your problem and you can't fix it. If you don't, the weight of it can grind you into the ground. Saying, 'F*ck it, it's not my problem' to someone is too harsh, but the sentiment is right.

SUPPORT, DON'T FIX

Support those who need it, but make a conscious choice not to try to solve their problems for them.

Step 1: The check-in
What happens when I take on people's problems?

How I respond when I see others struggling
___
___
___
___

Examples of when my support became self-sacrifice
___
___
___
___

What I think will happen if I don't help
___
___
___
___
___

Step 2: The shift
If I maintain boundaries and don't fix things for others ...

Ways I can support others without trying to fix their problem
___
___
___

The differences between 'empathy' and 'responsibility'
___
___
___

How I feel when I prioritize my own needs without feeling guilty
___
___
___

Now, create a list of situations where you might need to remind yourself: 'This is not my problem.'

___
___
___
___

F*CK IT
DOS AND DON'Ts

How to support someone (helpfully)

DO:

- ☑ Offer emotional support and follow through on that offer if needed.
- ☑ Encourage them to seek professional support if it could help with their problem.
- ☑ Listen, even if you don't share their views/opinions.
- ☑ Take care of yourself – helping others is draining.

DON'T:

- ☒ Become overly involved.
- ☒ Give your all to the detriment of your own physical or mental well-being.
- ☒ Feel guilty if you aren't able to provide practical help.
- ☒ Try to solve their problem (unless you're the tw*t who caused it).

F*CK IT FLOWCHART

Help out or step out?
Use to decide whether you're part of the problem or should just back off.

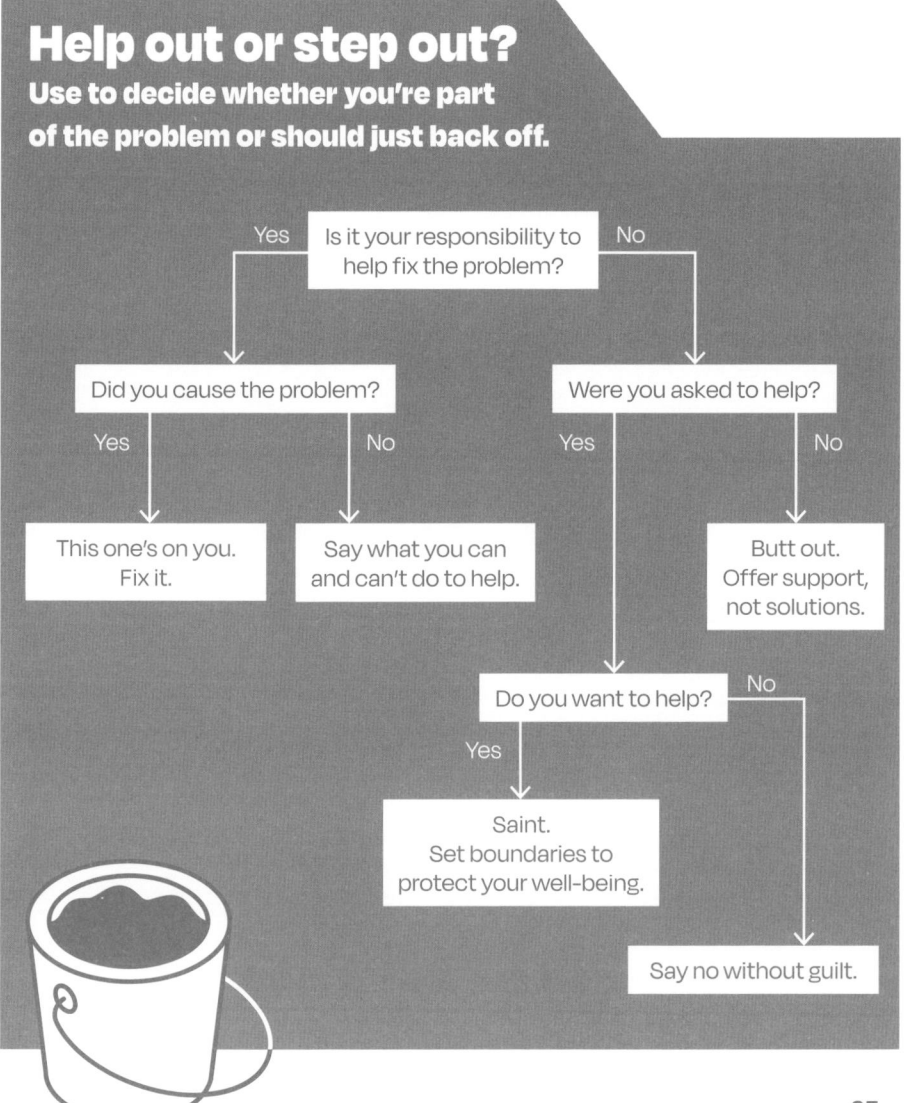

FILE A COMPLAINT

It pays to complain, right? Yes, in some situations. If you might get a well-deserved apology, complain away. Done well, you'll reap the benefits. But if it's going to be bloody stressful and no one's listening to you, you need to weigh up the pros and cons before you drive yourself into an early grave. If the stress outweighs the reward – f✲ck it, just walk away and move on.

WINNING OR WHINGING?

Don't introduce unnecessary stress into your life. Pick your battles (and choose your complaints wisely).

Step 1: The check-in
Am I comfortable with complaining?

When I complain, I feel

_____
_____
_____

Things I am most likely to complain about

_____
_____
_____

What I'm really trying to express when I complain

_____
_____
_____
_____
_____

Step 2: The shift
I know when to complain and when to let it go ...

What I can stop complaining about and instead take action
_____
_____

Long-held complaints I choose to put behind me
_____
_____

I could complain in a constructive way by
_____
_____

Choose one of your long-held complaints from the list above and consciously let it go.

I choose to let go of _____
because _____

When I let it go, it makes me feel _____
_____
_____
_____

F*CK IT TOP TIPS

Make your voice heard

* Be concise and stick to the facts/evidence.

* Don't lose your temper or make it personal. When you lose your temper, you lose the battle.

* Have a clear idea of what you're hoping to achieve (such as an apology, refund or change in behaviour). Suggest solutions.

* Sarcasm won't get you anywhere. Be polite, kind, respectful and sincere.

* Do you actually have a valid complaint or are you wasting everyone's time and getting stressed for nothing?

* Be patient. You might not get a resolution immediately, but boy, you'll feel better for saying something.

* Remember, if you're unhappy about something, you have the right to complain. Don't be scared to use that right.

F*CK IT FLOWCHART

Should I complain?
Use to decide whether you're on to a winner or are better off cutting your losses.

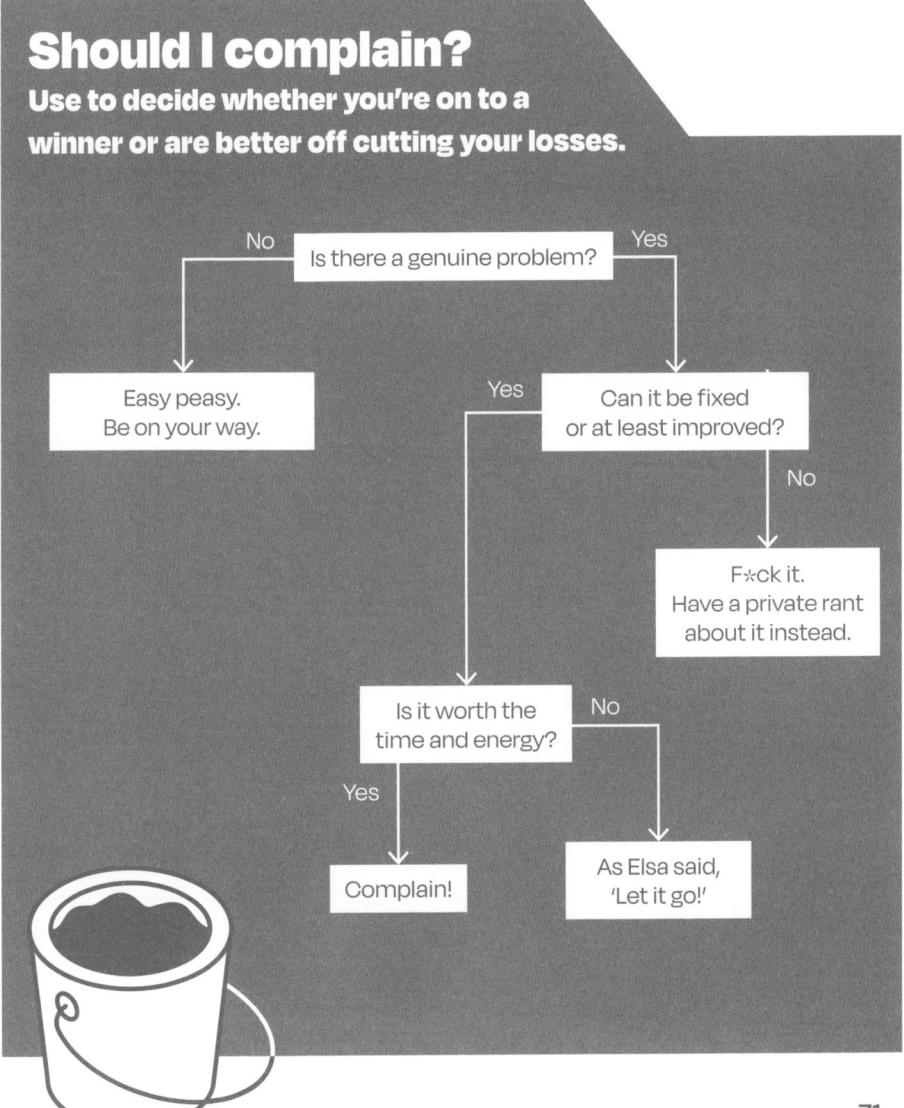

Is there a genuine problem?
- No → Easy peasy. Be on your way.
- Yes → Can it be fixed or at least improved?
  - Yes → Is it worth the time and energy?
    - Yes → Complain!
    - No → As Elsa said, 'Let it go!'
  - No → F*ck it. Have a private rant about it instead.

THE DATING GAME

Just one chapter on dating? It needs a whole book! Whatever your age, however 'experienced' you think you are, dating is described as a game for a reason. Rules, rewards, losses (and wins if you're lucky) – it's a bit like pin the tail on the donkey, but made even harder because the donkey keeps moving. You'll never get dating spot-on; the best you can do is learn to navigate it without throwing the towel in completely.

WHEN TWO BECOME ONE

Consider your motivations for being in a relationship and what you want out of it.

Step 1: The check-in
How is dating going for me?

My fears and worries about dating
_____
_____
_____

How I feel after a date
_____
_____
_____

Good and bad choices I've made
_____
_____
_____
_____
_____

Step 2: The shift
I have a clear idea about what I want from a relationship ...

My non-negotiables in a relationship
_____
_____
_____

A healthy, secure relationship looks/feels like this
_____
_____
_____

I'm in the dating game because
_____
_____
_____

Now, write down ten positive qualities you bring to a relationship.

_____	_____
_____	_____
_____	_____
_____	_____
_____	_____

F*CK IT
DOS AND DON'Ts

Date like a pro

DO:

- ☑ Know what you want from a relationship – but try to keep a degree of flexibility.
- ☑ Be positive. If you think of yourself as unlucky in love, you probably will be.
- ☑ Set and maintain your boundaries.
- ☑ Communicate, communicate, communicate – ask questions, express yourself!

DON'T:

- ☒ Be dishonest. Even harmless lies will come back to bite you on the bottom.
- ☒ Suppress who you are to keep another person happy.
- ☒ Overthink, especially in the early stages of a relationship.
- ☒ Ignore red flags – they're usually spot on.

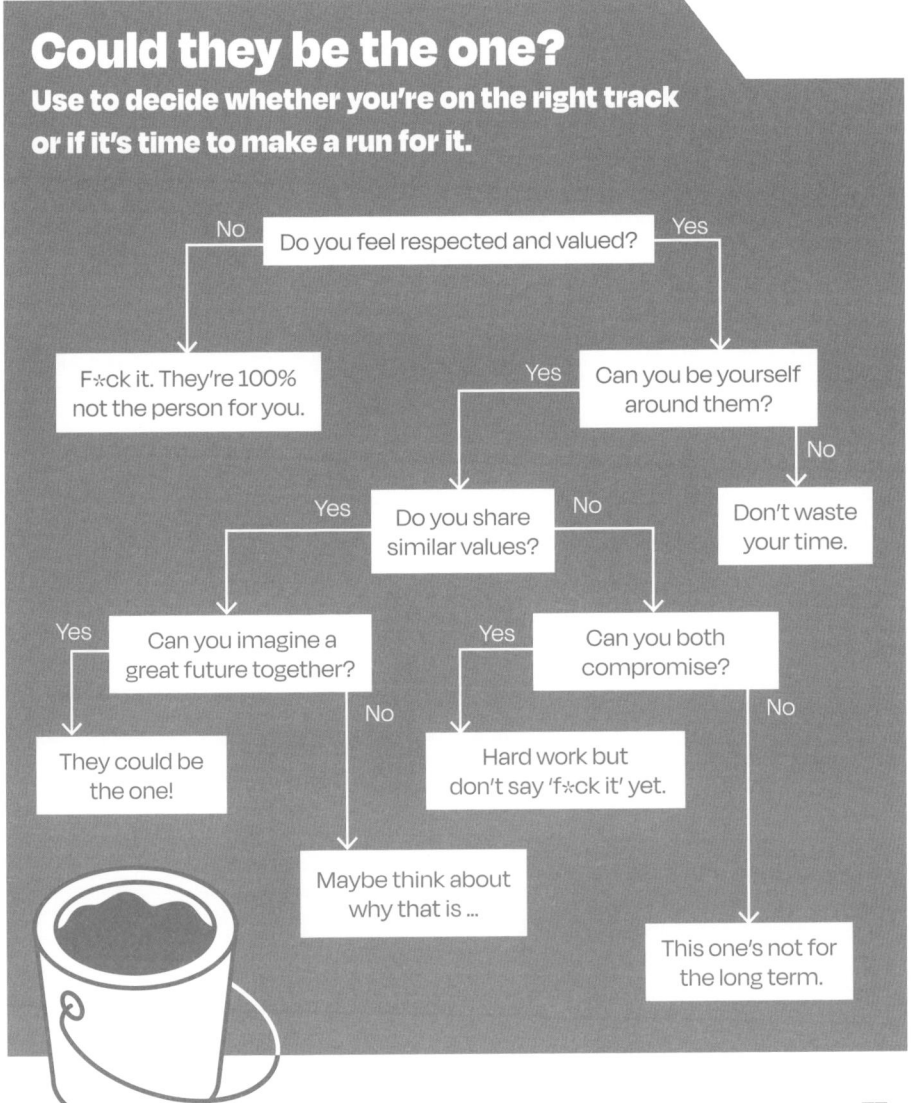

Does your heart leap when you receive an invitation? Or does your face drop?
Not everyone is a social beast. Even if you are, there are still times when you'd rather be at home in your PJs. Let's be honest, time is too precious to get roped in to things you don't want to do. And if something does float your boat, set aside your worries and go.
Be bold – ask yourself how YOU really want to spend YOUR time.

TAKE THE WORRY OUT OF RSVPS

What makes you deliberate when it comes to invitations? Aligning RSVPs with your values makes for less faffing about.

Step 1: The check-in
How does the current me react to invitations?

Emotions I feel when I get an invitation
___
___
___

Invitations that drain me
___
___
___

Reasons I've said yes to invitations I didn't want to accept
___
___
___
___

Step 2: The shift
When what I want becomes my main consideration ...

I can say no to an invitation without guilt when

Boundaries I need to set to protect my time and well-being

Invitations that energize me

A positive affirmation to support you.

> 'I choose to accept invitations that align with my joy and values and which support my well-being. I trust myself to say "yes" or "no" for the right reasons and to honour what is true to me.'

F*CK IT TOP TIPS

How to decline an invitation politely

You might be thinking, 'F*ck it, I'd rather be at home with a takeaway and *Love Island*,' but keep that to yourself. Yes, honesty and clarity are the best policy, but you also don't want to be struck off everyone's invitation list. To avoid ending up sad and extremely lonely, try these responses instead.

* 'That sounds great, but _____ isn't really my thing. How about dinner soon, though?'

* 'Thanks for inviting me. Unfortunately, I won't be able to make it but have a great time!'

* 'I don't really enjoy _____, so I'm going to sit this one out!'

* 'I'd love to _____, but I've been really busy lately and I've promised myself a quiet weekend.'

And the ultimate way to keep it simple:

* 'I'm sorry, I won't be able to make it.'

F*CK IT FLOWCHART

Should I stay or should I go?
Use to decide if something you're invited to is for the bucket or f*ck it list.

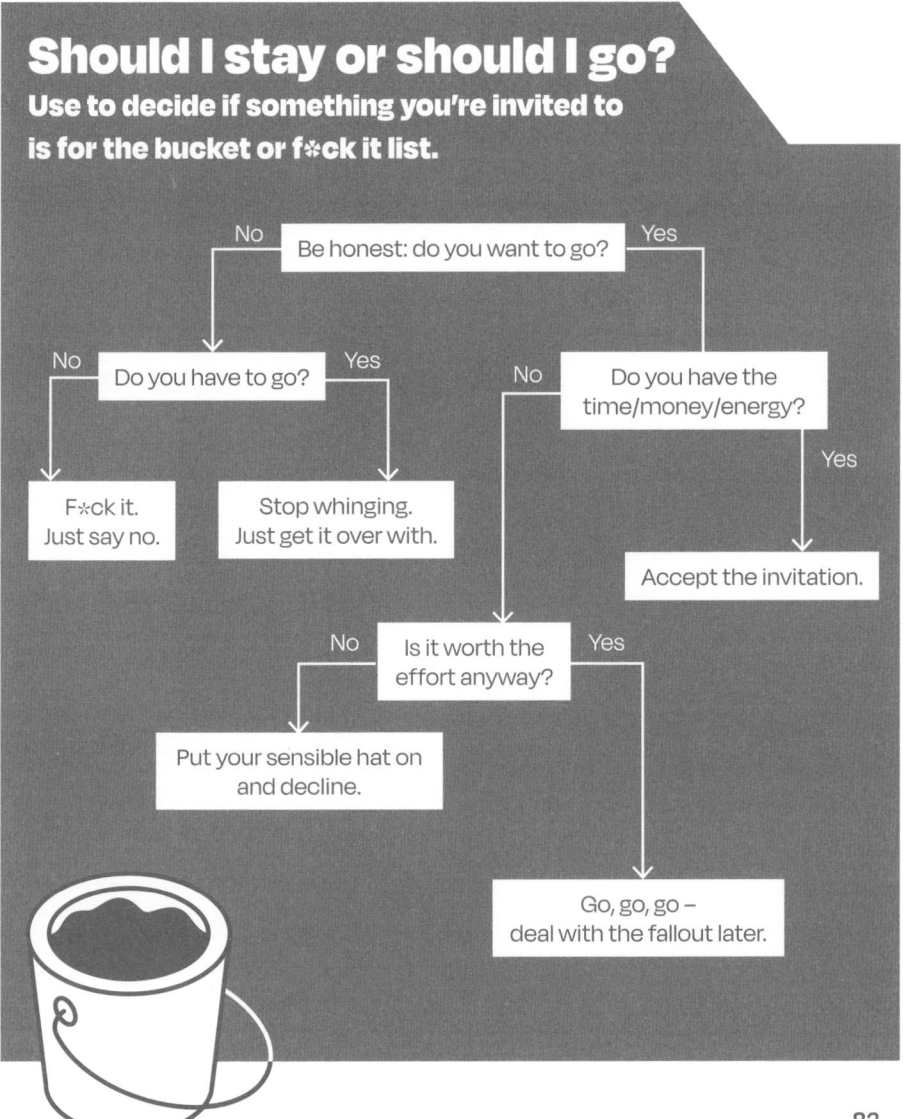

MESSAGE INCOMING

You sit down to watch a film and ... PING!
You're in the middle of a delicious dream and ... PING! You know the story. You've let text, email and social media notifications take over your life. The good news is it's never too late to say 'f∗ck it' and silence your devices. Although, if you're thoroughly addicted, you'll need to put some hard graft in.

YOUR DIGITAL WELL-BEING

An unhealthy relationship with digital devices causes stress, an inability to focus and general brain drain. Save yourself by stepping back into the real world.

Step 1: The check-in
The impact the digital world has on my life ...

How I feel when I hear a notification
_____
_____
_____

What I think will happen if I ignore messages
_____
_____
_____

Information overload makes me feel
_____
_____
_____
_____

Step 2: The shift
What taking charge of my relationship with my devices looks like ...

If I stop checking notifications, I can use the time to
_____
_____
_____

The boundaries I can put in place around email/social media
_____
_____
_____
_____

How I feel when I disconnect from the digital world
_____
_____
_____
_____

Set yourself a clear boundary to create a healthy relationship with tech.

'I commit to only spend _____ minutes _____ times a day checking my devices.'

F*CK IT
DOS AND DON'Ts

Build a healthy relationship with the digital world

DO:

- ☑ Turn off non-essential notifications.
- ☑ Try switching off all your digital devices for 24 hours. Eek – you can do it, even if it's just one day every fortnight.
- ☑ Put your digital devices out of sight and reach. Schedule in non-digital time to rediscover the neglected hobbies you love.

DON'T:

- ☒ Feel compelled to respond to messages immediately. Be available on your terms.
- ☒ Prioritize digital connections over real-world connections.
- ☒ Keep digital devices in your bedroom. Scrolling through cat videos is soothing, but it doesn't beat a good night's sleep.

F*CK IT FLOWCHART

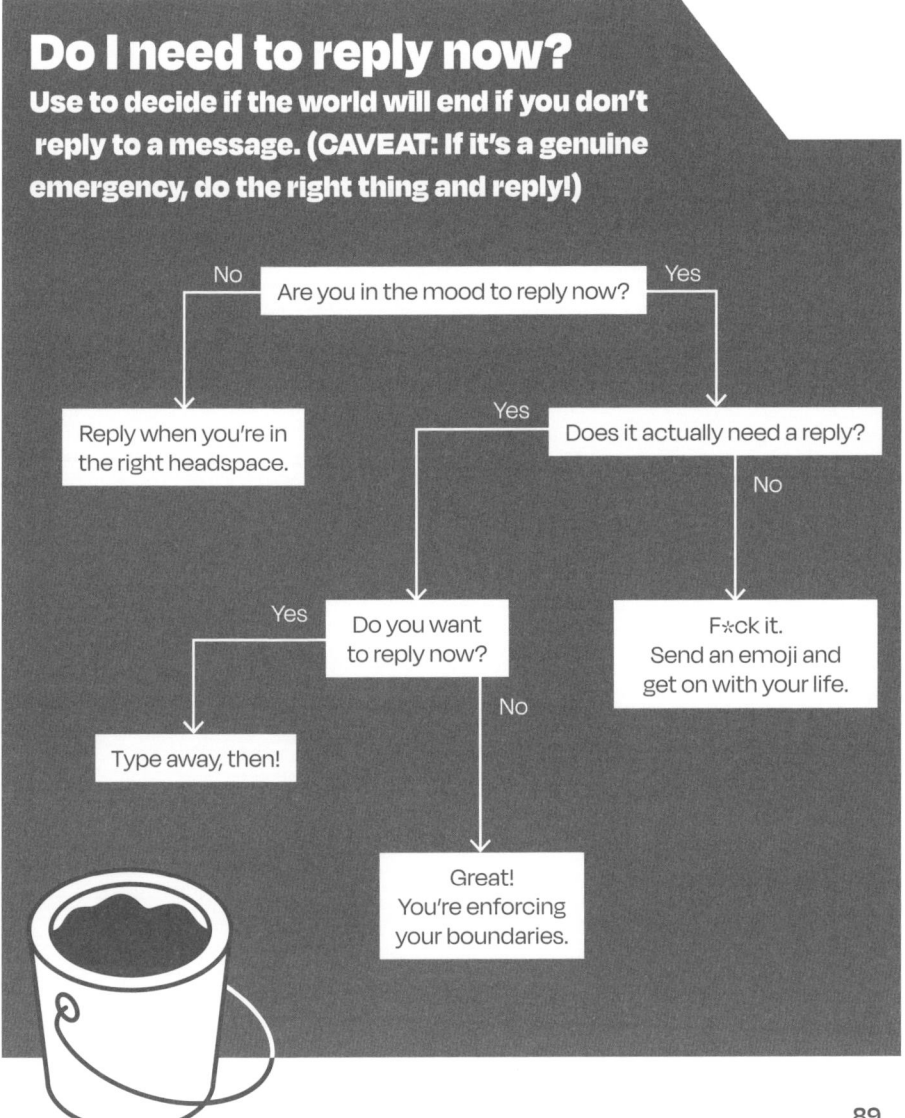

EMBRACE FAILURE

What's the worst that could happen?
That's the rational question to ask yourself, but how often is it the first thing that comes to mind? Taking on a challenge, trying something new, pushing boundaries – there's a risk of it not going as you expected. In reality, there's no such thing as failing, just lessons to learn. So, embrace those bumps on the road and say 'f*ck it' to failure.

GROWTH OVER FAILURE

So-called failure can knock you hard if you let it. The solution? Don't let it.

Step 1: The check-in
How do thoughts of failure impact me?

How I feel when something doesn't go as well as I wanted
_____
_____
_____

Past failures I still dwell on
_____
_____
_____

A failure that made me feel more determined
_____
_____
_____
_____

Step 2: The shift
If I choose to accept that a failure is a learning opportunity ...

What I would say to a friend who thought they'd failed

Words I can use to pick myself up and carry on

What I learn when I stumble

Choose something you thought was a failure and list the positives that came out of it.

F*CK IT TOP TIPS

Positive approaches to failure

* It's okay to feel bad for a bit. Work through those feelings, then say 'f*ck it' and move on.

* Bin negative thoughts and put positive ones in your bucket. For example, 'This didn't go well, but I know how to make it work next time.'

* Talk! Getting someone else's thoughts can put things in perspective.

* When something goes wrong, make sure you accept an appropriate level of responsibility. Don't beat yourself up if the failure was caused by something outside your control.

* Failure isn't a step backward. It's an opportunity to move forward, having grown wiser.

* Do something to relax and reduce your stress levels – don't punish yourself.

F*CK IT FLOWCHART

Have I failed?
Use to turn a crock of sh*t into a pot of gold.
(But be realistic – keep in mind how long you want
to keep trying before you concede defeat and say 'f*ck it'.)

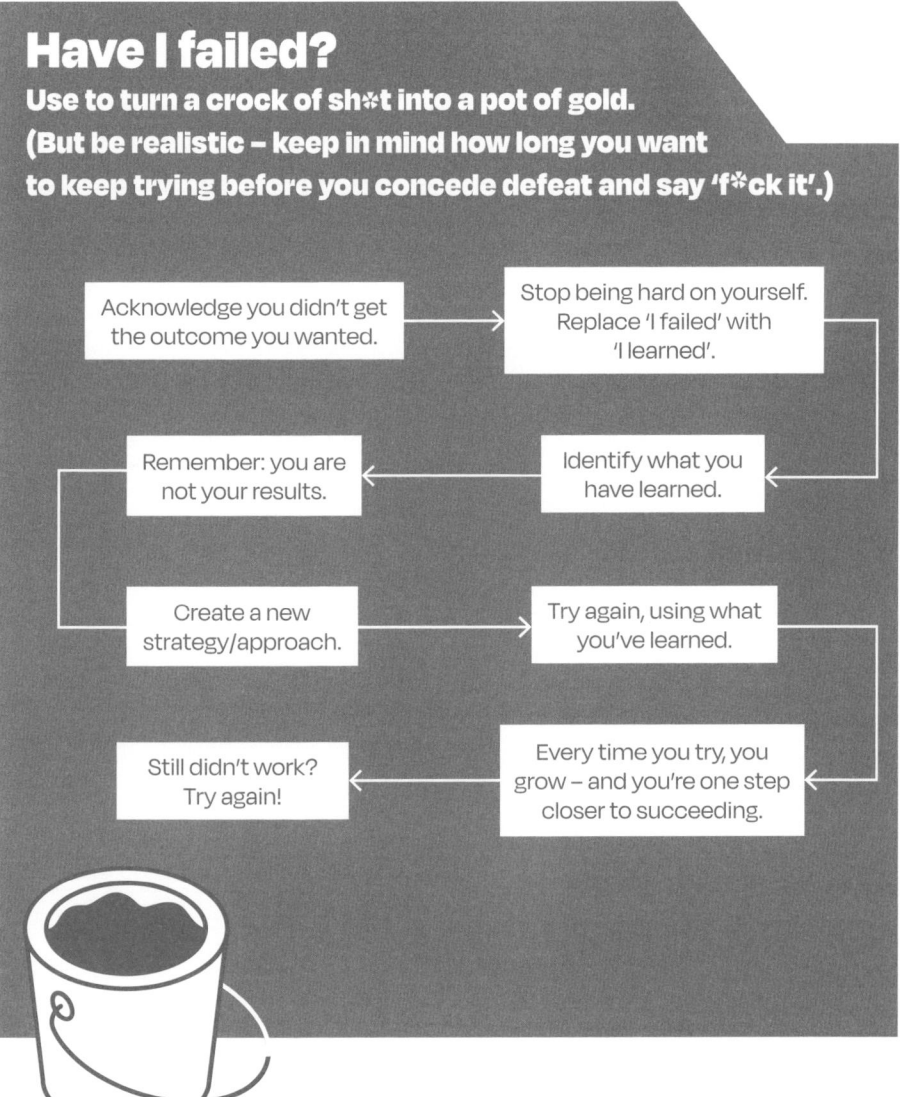

Acknowledge you didn't get the outcome you wanted. → Stop being hard on yourself. Replace 'I failed' with 'I learned'. → Identify what you have learned. → Remember: you are not your results. → Create a new strategy/approach. → Try again, using what you've learned. → Every time you try, you grow – and you're one step closer to succeeding. → Still didn't work? Try again!

IN PURSUIT OF PERFECTION

No one is perfect. You might want to be, but you're setting yourself up for unnecessary stress. Putting constant pressure on yourself has implications for your mental and physical health (think low self-esteem, anxiety, high blood pressure – all the nasties). Yet we still do it! Making mistakes is part of human nature. If you're not making them, are you human at all?

GOOD ENOUGH OVER PERFECTION

Don't waste your time striving for the impossible. Quit putting pressure on yourself and you'll enjoy life more.

Step 1: The check-in
How is trying to be perfect bringing me down?

Expectations I place on myself
_____
_____
_____

Expectations I think other people have of me
_____
_____
_____

Ways I compare myself to others
_____
_____
_____
_____

Step 2: The shift
If I was happy to be 'good enough' ...

When I accept that 'okay' is enough, I feel

Impossibly high standards I can lower

Positive words I would use to describe myself (and replace the negative self-talk)

An affirmation to support your journey:

'I am proud of my efforts and progress, even if the outcome isn't perfect.'

F*CK IT TOP TIPS

Top ways to let go of perfection

* Be aware of your perfectionist tendencies so you can see when they're happening (and can tell them to f*ck off).

* Focus on positives. For every 'bad' thing, find three good things.

* Be kind to yourself – allow yourself to make mistakes.

* Set reasonable and achievable goals for yourself.

* Accept criticism – don't take it personally. Healthy criticism can help you do better.

* Put less pressure on yourself. Be proud of working hard and doing your best.

* If something brings you joy, it doesn't matter if it's not done perfectly.

* Quit procrastinating – a rough start is better than no start at all.

F*CK IT FLOWCHART

Is it good enough?
Use to reduce perfectionism – it's overrated.

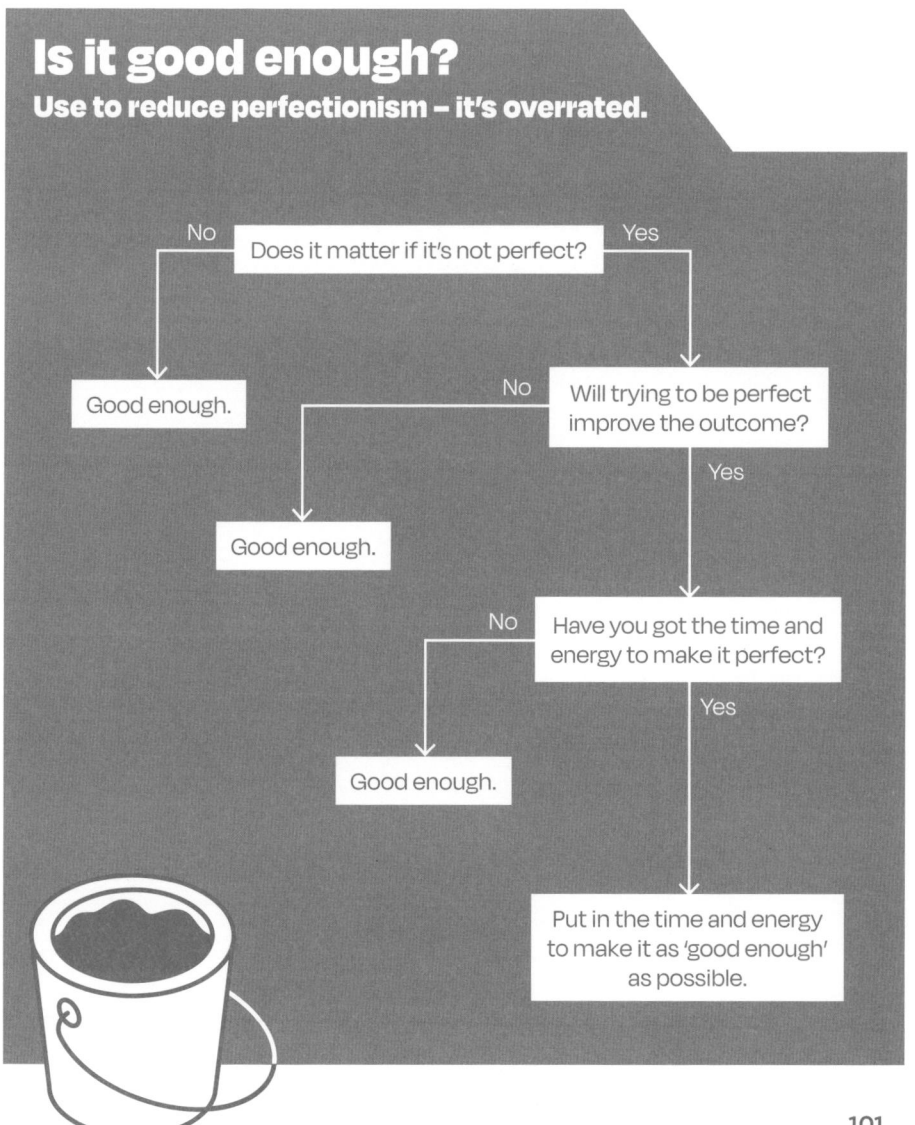

Humans are sociable animals, and we're hardwired to connect with other people. We don't want to be rejected and we therefore have a self-induced fear of being judged for being different. We believe that fitting in will make us happier. Should you hide who you are because you're worried people won't like you? Or should you say 'f*ck it', be yourself and connect with those people who accept you for the brilliant individual you are?

WALK YOUR OWN PATH

Define your own strengths – don't let other people's expectations do it for you.

Step 1: The check-in
What am I doing just to be part of the flock?

Parts of myself I feel pressure to hide in order to belong
_____
_____
_____

When I don't fit in, I feel
_____
_____
_____

Feeling like I need to fit in is holding me back from
_____
_____
_____
_____

Step 2: The shift
If I embrace my true self and stop fearing rejection ...

Situations where I most feel myself

Three things that make me unique

When I feel I should try to fit in, I want my inner voice to say

Use your responses above to write a reminder to be proud of who you are.

I will not try to fit in if it makes me feel

Instead, I celebrate that I am

F*CK IT DOs AND DON'Ts

A quick guide to being yourself

DO:

- ☑ Embrace your own individuality. It's easy to be like everyone else, but nowhere near as fun as being you.
- ☑ Find your tribe. Plenty of people out there share your values and interests.
- ☑ Challenge your comfort zone. You'll discover more about yourself and build your confidence in being you.

DON'T:

- ☒ Forget your own worth. Your value is not defined by the approval of others.
- ☒ Be afraid to walk away from situations/people where you're not comfortable being yourself.
- ☒ Let fear of not fitting in stop you from trying new experiences and meeting new people.

F*CK IT FLOWCHART

Is this the place for me?
Use to decide whether a situation celebrates or denigrates you.

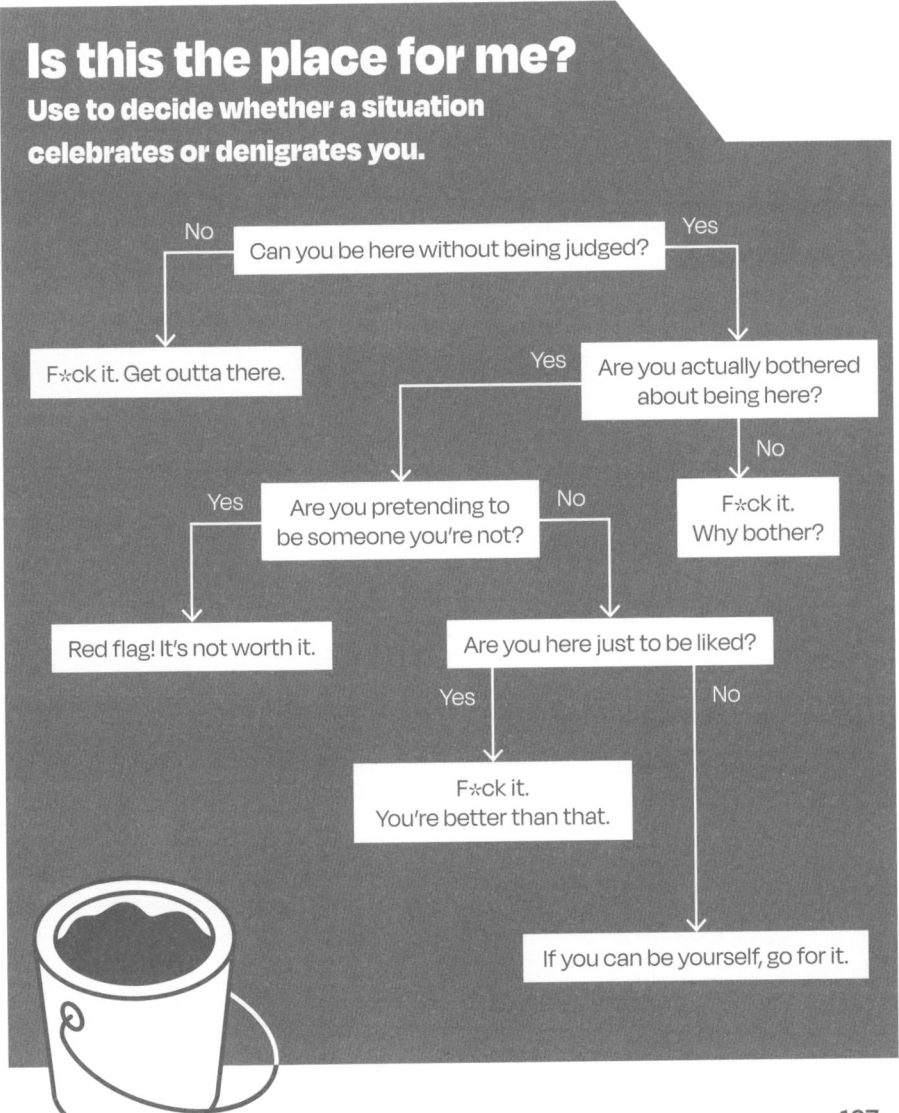

Do you know someone who is brilliant at saying no? You won't find them stuck in the office trying to meet an impossible deadline while everyone else is in the bar round the corner. Sadly, most people struggle to say no without feeling the need to explain, lie or worry about what other people think. 'No' is a tiny word with a mighty impact. When you make it work for you, it's one of the most powerful tools you have.

THE POWER OF NO

Do you find yourself saying 'yes' more often than 'no'? Time to redress the balance.

Step 1: The check-in
What's the worst that could happen if I just say 'no'?

What I worry will happen if I say 'no'
_____
_____
_____
_____

What I imagine people think of me when I say 'no'
_____
_____
_____
_____

How saying 'yes' too often affects me
_____
_____
_____
_____

Step 2: The shift
If I felt confident about saying 'no' ...

How being comfortable saying 'no' benefits my well-being

_____
_____
_____

My boundaries are important to me because

_____
_____
_____

How I feel inside when I say 'no' confidently and with compassion

_____
_____

Think of a situation in the coming week when you can practise saying 'no'. How can you prepare for it?

_____
_____
_____
_____

F*CK IT
DOs AND DON'Ts

Say 'no' – and mean it

DO:

- ☑ Actually use the word 'no'! Say it loud and proud, not sandwiched between umms, ahhs and explanations.

- ☑ Think before you give your answer. For example, would saying 'no' to your boss be career suicide? Sometimes, you need to wear your sensible hat.

- ☑ Be clear and firm. This shuts down any opportunities to be persuaded.

DON'T:

- ☒ Feel the need to explain your response in great detail – short and sweet is fine.

- ☒ Feel guilty. Saying 'no' is an act of self-care, not selfishness.

- ☒ Change your mind just to keep someone else happy. If they can't accept 'no', stick to your guns and walk away.

F*CK IT FLOWCHART

Can I say 'no' to this?
Use when you need to set your boundaries and decide whether it's okay to say 'no'.

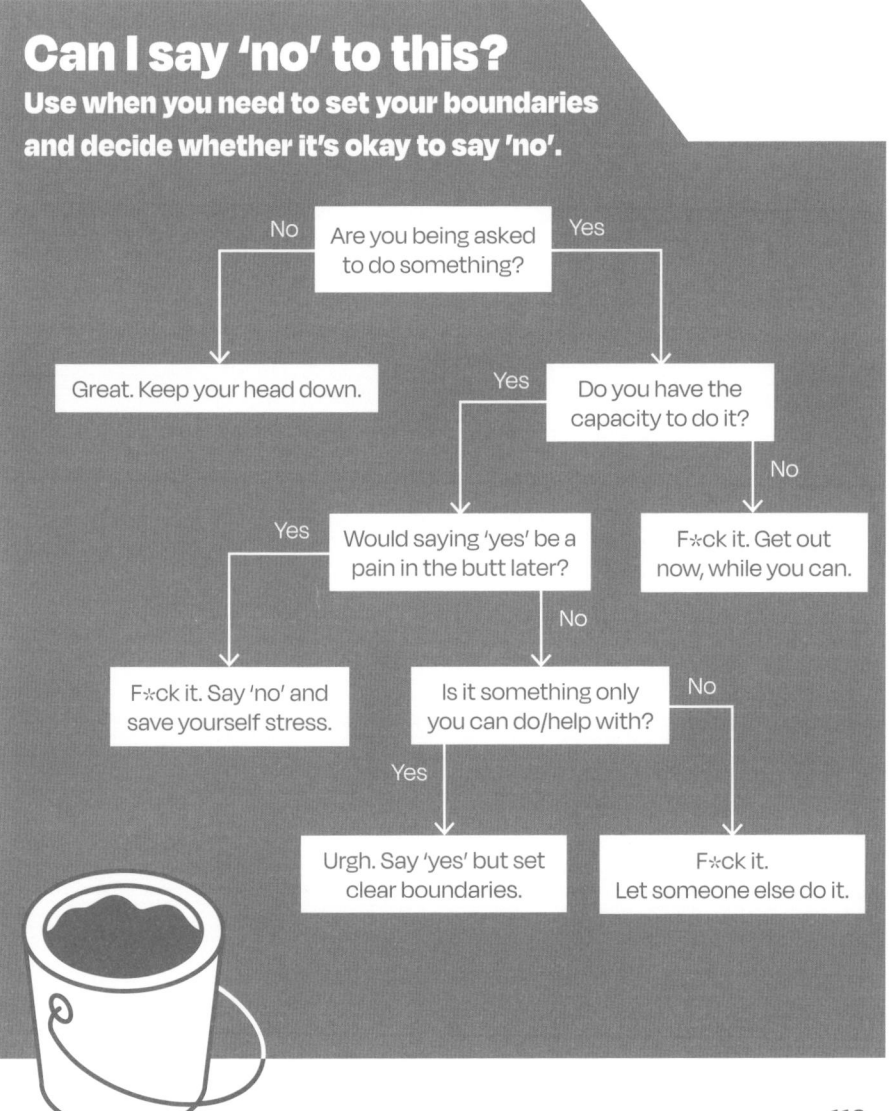

THE LAST WORD

Do you always feel compelled to have the last word? Have a think about whether that's good for you. It might give you a buzz in the moment, but it achieves very little except maybe making you look a bit of a kn✶b. Remember, that feel-good moment is fleeting. It's far better to know when to say 'f✶ck it' and move on. More often than not, that's the best option.

LISTEN, DON'T CONTROL

There are more important things than winning if you want a conversation to have a positive outcome.

Step 1: The check-in
How do I try to control conversations?

How I feel when someone else gets the last word
_____
_____
_____

Situations where I feel most triggered to 'win' an argument
_____
_____
_____

How others might feel when I control a conversation
_____
_____
_____
_____

Step 2: The shift
When I let go of trying to have the last word ...

How it feels to truly listen to others

What I gain by letting someone else have the last word

How my relationships will improve

What can you do to check yourself next time you feel the urge to have the last word?

F*CK IT
DOS AND DON'Ts

How to have a constructive argument

Clashes of interests, personal preferences, arguments about facts – these can all be managed better when you argue constructively. And you're more likely to get a positive outcome.

DO:

- ☑ Be fair and give the other person a chance to think/respond.
- ☑ Be empathetic – try to understand why the other person thinks the way they do.
- ☑ Stay rational. If you feel yourself getting emotional, take a few deep breaths.
- ☑ Accept when you're wrong. And if it's the other way round – be a gracious winner.

DON'T:

- ☒ Raise your voice, lose your temper or talk over other people.
- ☒ Make it personal.
- ☒ Refuse to listen. You may not agree with them but do acknowledge the other person's point of view.

F*CK IT FLOWCHART

Should I try to have the last word?

Use to analyse whether you should take an argument to its bitter end or withdraw before you make yourself look like a tw*t.

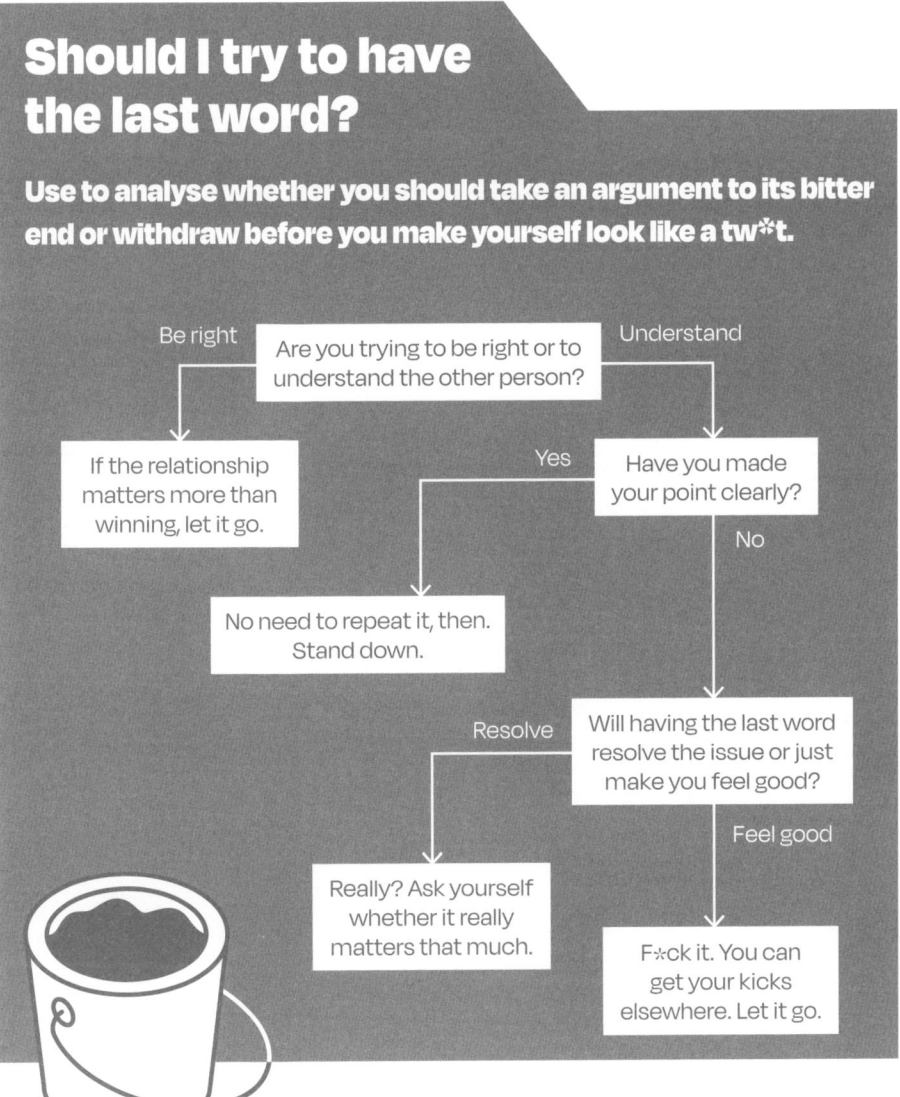

WHAT NEXT?

Whether you've dipped in and out of this book or worked through from start to finish, you're making brilliant progress toward ditching the dead weight in your life. You've learned valuable lessons about how to do things differently and what to let go of, prioritize and embrace for a healthier, happier life. As the great Bruce Lee said, 'If you spend too much time thinking about a thing, you'll never get it done.' Now's the time to put everything you've learned into action!

TEN THINGS I'M GOING TO SAY 'F*CK IT' TO IMMEDIATELY

For example: putting other people's needs ahead of my own ...

1. _____
2. _____
3. _____
4. _____
5. _____
6. _____
7. _____
8. _____
9. _____
10. _____

TEN THINGS I'M GOING TO PUT IN MY BUCKET AND EMBRACE

For example: taking time to discover new things and pursue exciting interests ...

1. _____

2. _____

3. _____

4. _____

5. _____

6. _____

7. _____

8. _____

9. _____

10. _____

TEN BELIEFS I'M GOING TO DITCH

For example: the need to have the last word; feeling bad about saying no ...

1.
2.
3.
4.
5.
6.
7.
8.
9.
10.

TEN BOUNDARIES I WILL PUT IN PLACE TO LOOK AFTER MY WELL-BEING

For example: time for me; how I respond to other people's demands ...

1.
2.
3.
4.
5.
6.
7.
8.
9.
10.

TEN THINGS I WANT TO ACHIEVE FOR MYSELF IN THE NEXT YEAR

For example: find a job I love; learn how to do something new ...

1. _____
2. _____
3. _____
4. _____
5. _____
6. _____
7. _____
8. _____
9. _____
10. _____

TEN WAYS I WANT MY LIFE TO HAVE CHANGED IN A YEAR'S TIME

For example: have a strong circle of non-toxic friends; no longer living my life based on what-ifs ...

1.
2.
3.
4.
5.
6.
7.
8.
9.
10.

'Life isn't about finding yourself. Life is about creating yourself.'

George Bernard Shaw